Muslim scientists

IBN AL-BAITAR
Doctor of Natural Medicine

Published by Ali Gator Productions
Copyright © 2021 Ali Gator Productions, Second Edition,
First Published 2017

National Library of Australia Cataloguing–in-Publication (CIP) data:
Ahmed Imam
ISBN: 978-1-921772-39-9
For primary school age, Juvenile fiction, Dewey Number: 823.92

Adapted from the original title Ilmuan Muslim Ibnu Al-Baitsar first published by Pelangi Mizan.
Copyright © 2015 by Author Risma Dewi, Illustrator Nano. Printed in Indonesia.

T: +61 (3) 9386 2771
P.O. Box 2536, Regent West, Melbourne Victoria, 3072 Australia
E: info@ali-gator.com **W:** www.ali-gator.com

W0038521

بِسْمِ اللهِ الرَّحْمٰنِ الرَّحِيمِ

BISMILLAHIR RAHMANIR RAHIM

IN THE NAME OF ALLAH, MOST GRACIOUS, MOST MERCIFUL

Inspiring our children to learn about
the great Muslim scientists, scholars
and adventurers from
the Golden Age of Islam.

2

NOTES TO PARENTS AND TEACHERS

The Muslim Scientists Series aims to introduce to young readers some of the famous Muslim scientists, scholars and adventurers who discovered and invented many things that we use today and take for granted.

It is our hope that young children will be inspired by these amazing people and be encouraged to pursue their own path of discovery and questioning. It all starts with a passion for learning.

Whilst reading about Ibn Al-Baitar, "Doctor of Natural Medicine", talk to the children about what they do when they get sick. Do they go to the Doctor ? Do they know of any plants that can help them get better naturally ? Have they ever heard of "Tibb An-Nabawi" - Medicine of the Prophet.

Have they ever planted anything and watched it grow ? What types of fruit do they know grow on plants or trees ? Have they ever eaten honey ? Do they know what black seeds are ? Have they ever eaten dates ? So many questions for young minds to contemplate.

In Sha Allah (God Willing) if this series helps to inspire our young readers to be the next generation of thinkers, to better mankind through inventions and discoveries, then we have truly met our goal.

Ibn Al-Baitar was born in 1197 in Malaga, Spain.

At this time Spain was a thriving Muslim region known as, Al Andalus, or Islamic Spain.

Al Andalus was an exciting place to be. There were many great thinkers and scientists throughout the region.

6

From an early age Ibn Al-Baitar became interested in learning about plants and how they could be used for making medicines.

He was inspired by The Prophet Muhammad (PBUH) who said in a Hadith, "for every disease there is a cure."*

Ibn Al-Baitar wanted to find these cures.

He would sit with the "Botanists", the people who study the science of plants and learn from them.

* Sahih Bukhari

HADITH - SAYING OF
THE PROPHET MUHAMMAD (PBUH)

PBUH – PEACE BE UPON HIM

So as to learn more about plants, Ibn Al-Baitar decided to journey outside of Europe.

He went to Africa and Asia where he came across all kinds of plants that no one in Europe had ever seen before.

Ibn Al-Baitar was truly amazed with the beauty and variety of Allah's creations.

When Ibn Al-Baitar visited Egypt, the Sultan heard about
a man with great knowledge of plants and
wanted to meet with him.

Once the Sultan met Ibn Al-Baitar he was so impressed with
Ibn Al-Baitar he invited him to stay and be in charge of
all the plants and medicines across all of Egypt.

This was a great opportunity for Ibn Al-Baitar
as the Nile valley was rich with vegetation.

11

12

After Egypt, Ibn Al-Baitar's next adventure was in Damascus, Syria.

Here he followed the advice of the Prophet Muhammad (PBUH) and used Black Seed, Honey, Dates and other types of herbs to treat the sick.

Ibn Al-Baitar's knowledge of natural medicines was increasing year by year.

Through his research and study
Ibn Al-Baitar found over 300 kinds of plants
that could be made into medicine.

These medicines could be used
to treat all kinds of diseases, especially
those related to the head,
eyes and ears.

To share his knowledge with the world
Ibn Al-Baitar wrote a great book.

It has over 1400 listings of plants, foods,
and medicines and their uses.

This detailed book has so much information
that it has been translated from Arabic
into German and French.

Ibn Al-Baitar's was famous for many things.
He was a Botanist (someone who studies plants),
a Pharmacist (knowing what medicine to give people),
and a Doctor (helping to cure the sick).

Yet most of all, he was famous for all the
natural medicines he discovered.

Ibn Al-Baitar was truly an amazing man.

19

Ibn Al-Baitar was inspired
by the Prophet Muhammad's (PBUH)
knowledge of the cures available in plants
and natural medicines.

He understood that these are all
blessings from Allah.

Ibn Al-Baitar knew that if he studied
about plants to gain Allah's pleasure,
it would be an act of Ibadah – Worship.

PBUH – PEACE BE UPON HIM

20

During all his years of research and study, Ibn Al-Baitar
knew that all the answers he was ever looking for
were in the Qur'an and in the Sunnah.

And we should too.

SUNNAH - EXAMPLE OF THE PROPHET MUHAMMAD (PBUH)
PBUH – PEACE BE UPON HIM

الْحَمْدُ لِلَّٰهِ

ALHAMDULILLAH - PRAISE BE TO ALLAH

When we are going to learn something new,
we should ask Allah for guidance,
just like the Prophet Muhammad (PBUH) did.
He would say :

اَللّٰهُمَّ اِنِّي اَسْئَلُكَ عِلْمًا نَافِعًا

Allah Humma Innee As'aluka Ilman Naafi'aan.

"Allah! I ask You for knowledge
That will benefit me"

PBUH - PEACE BE UPON HIM